M000026030

"We sometimes think that kindness is a weakness in competitive situations. But in this beautiful book, *The ROI of Kindness,* Brian Biro and Mac Anderson show us the deeper truth, that there is a secret power to kindness."

JOHN ROBBINS
Best-selling author, President of 600,000-member Food Revolution Network

"Wow…if you are interested in putting a little more kindness in your culture, this is a must read! It tells how companies like Southwest Airlines, Chick-fil-a, and Starbucks have done it, and become leaders in their industry."

VIC CONANT
CEO Nightingale Conant

"There are hundreds of books on leadership, selling, teamwork and service, but this is a first on how kindness can impact your bottom line. I loved it!"

IRA BLUMENTHAL
President of Pat Summitt Leadership Group, Best Selling Author

"I can't remember the last time that I read a book and immediately thought, this is a must read for every employee in our company!"
HENRY BEDFORD
Chairman Southwestern Family of Companies

"Creating a culture of kindness in your company will offer rewards that will not only increase your bottom line, and more importantly cultivate a heartbeat of positivity in your organization. This book is a powerful reminder that kindness is what really matters to people."
ROBIN CROW
CEO Dark Horse Studio, Best Selling Author

THE ROI OF KINDNESS™

THE SURPRISING SECRET THAT GENERATES LONG-TERM RESULTS

Brian Biro and Mac Anderson

Copyright © 2020 by Inspire Kindness

Published by Inspire Kindness, Inc.,
a Member of Southwestern Family of Companies
2451 Atrium Way
Nashville, TN 37214

Inspire Kindness is a registered trademark.

Printed and bound in the United States of America.
ISBN 978-0-578-62760-1

inspirekindness.com
hello@inspirekindness.com
877-935-6357

Book design: Rich Nickel, Elevate Creative

All rights reserved. No portion of this publication may be reproduced, stored
in a retrieval system or transmitted in any form by any means – except for brief
quotations in printed reviews – without the prior written permission of the
publisher.

WOZ 10 9 8 7 6 5 4 3 2

THE ROI OF KINDNESS™

THE SURPRISING SECRET THAT GENERATES LONG-TERM RESULTS

INTRODUCTION

I've been very blessed in my life as an entrepreneur. In those forty years I have learned a lot, and along the way I had the privilege of meeting many amazing people who were a lot smarter than me.

But, when I started to think about hanging up my entrepreneurial pursuits, I came to realize that retirement was not in the cards. I found myself searching for something that would bring me joy, where I could make a positive difference in the world.

And...I found it! Two years ago, I purchased the name *InspireKindness.com* and recently launched our own website where you can find powerful kindness stories and videos. We also feature over 100 proprietary kindness products where most importantly, a percentage of sales goes to our **Kindness for Kids Foundation,** which funds kindness campaigns for grade schools. Our goals are big, but our mission is simple… to start a kindness movement that will have a ripple effect around the world.

I truly believe that more than any other time in my life, more kindness in our schools, our homes, and our businesses is the answer to creating a better world. And, driven by this purpose and passion, the focus of this book is on kindness in the corporate world.

No one would argue that more kindness makes for a more pleasant work environment. However, no one has set out to prove with statistics and facts that **a culture of kindness can dramatically impact the bottom line.** And, companies like Starbucks, Kaiser Permanente, Southwest Airlines, Chick-fil-A, Zappos, Tom's, and

Disney.are shining examples of how they have become leaders in their industries by focusing on the most powerful secret to long-term business success.

How did they do it?
That's what this little book is all about!

Although I had the ROI of Kindness idea over a year ago, I knew I needed help to bring it to life. Therefore, I recruited JB Training out of Chicago to do the research on how a culture of kindness helps companies recruit and retain their best people. And they found what inevitably follows are loyal customers who become raving fans. From this research I'm proud to say we've developed a dynamic keynote speech, a workshop, and a webinar around the ROI of Kindness, not to merely talk about how kindness impacts the bottom line, but to prove it.

To help write this book I recruited my friend Brian Biro. He's a terrific writer (14 books) and a great speaker (rated one of the top 50 in the world) and he's one of the kindest people I've met. As the founder of **Simple Truths,** we published over 150 books and I'm proud to say many of them have sold over 500,000 copies. I had the honor of reading every manuscript from authors like Ken Blanchard, John Maxwell, Brian Tracy, Zig Ziglar, Stephen Covey, and many others.

Though I always enjoyed reading these positive, forward-thinking manuscripts, when I read one that spoke to my soul I always got 'goosebumps.' Brian's manuscript for the ROI of Kindness was definitely one of those! I loved it, and hope you will too.

Our goal is simple...to help you reach yours by putting a little more kindness in your culture.

And, by doing so, you'll make your people happier, your customers happier, and make the world a better place.

Enjoy!

Mac Anderson
Founder, **Inspire Kindness**
Also founder of McCord Travel, Successories, and Simple Truths

CHAPTER

1

THE GREATEST **OBSTACLE** TO DISCOVERING **THE TRUTH** IS THE BELIEF THAT YOU **ALREADY** KNOW IT

Question:

What color is a yield sign?

f you're like 95% of the over half a million participants in my events over the past 29 years, your immediate answer was **YELLOW.**

Over 45 years ago the USA switched to the international signage standards, and every yield sign you've seen for more than 45 years is **NOT** yellow…

It's red and white! It looks exactly like this:

You've seen thousands of yield signs. You see the same yield signs every day if you drive a similar route to a similar location. And you haven't seen **ONE** of them for what's right there in front of you! WHY?

The simple, but profound answer is at the heart of the magic in this book. It can open exciting new possibilities in your life, your work, your family, your health…. in **YOU.**

Why don't we see yield signs for what they are even when they're right in front of us?

IT'S BECAUSE
WE RARELY USE OUR
VISION
TO SEE

You know what we use instead?
We use our **MEMORY** and our **CONDITIONING.**

And whenever we use our memory to see, we do not see what IS. We see what WAS! And the second we lock on to what was, guess what we block out? We stop ourselves from seeing what IS and what **COULD BE!**

That's well and good for yield signs. And, I hope you'll all join me because this just might be the secret to wiping out road rage! You see, I'm the happiest driver I know! Why? Because every time I see a Yield sign I start cracking up! I think to myself: "What else have I been missing lately?" (And let me warn you, for the next couple of weeks, every time you drive by a yield sign it will feel like it jumps right out of the cement and smacks you on the back of the head).

So, where does it really matter to no longer depend upon your memory to see? It all comes down to one word:

PEOPLE.

Change the way you look at PEOPLE, the people you look at **Change.**

Change the way you see YOURSELF, the self you see will **Change.**

Change the way you see your CULTURE, the culture that determines your future will **Change.**

Let me show how powerful this opening to vision can be in your life. When my oldest daughter, Kelsey, came home from college the first time for Thanksgiving holiday, I finally realized how long – though I love her completely – I'd been staring at her as if she was an old **YELLOW** yield sign. I'd been looking at her as if she was still my little 11-year-old daughter! Hey, she'd been driving her own car for two-and-a-half years. She had been waking up hundreds and hundreds of miles away from us each day and deciding what she would do with the greatest gift she was ever given…. called **TODAY.**

She walked in the door that afternoon, a smile the size of North Carolina, and proceeded to announce to her mother and I that she already applied to and had already been accepted to do a very special service program in Ghana, in Africa… because Kelsey wants to make the world **BETTER.**

I looked at my daughter that day, maybe for the very first time. And, I finally broke through. I finally realized that every time I looked at her as if she was an old yellow yield sign, every time I used my MEMORY to see, what happened to our relationship? It went BACK-WARDS until I looked at the wisdom, courage, and kindness…at the remarkable woman that was standing right in front of me.

TODAY IT IS TIME FOR US TO USE OUR

VISION

to see the single-most important ingredient in build-ing an unstoppable culture in your organization. One that transforms every measure of success… from ROI, to retention, to service excellence, to brand power, to maximizing the buying experience for your customers, to attracting talent, to thriving on change, to becoming an incredible place to work.

CHAPTER

2

THE
ShhhECRET

s there truly a magical ingredient that can transform your culture, your team's consistent level of engagement, and your bottom line? Surely, such an elixir must be a fantasy. It could not be so simple, so strikingly clear, and so unassailably true for it not to be front and center in business today. It couldn't be…could it?

THEN AGAIN, YIELD SIGNS COULDN'T REALLY BE RED AND WHITE, COULD THEY?

Just for fun imagine, what if there **WAS** an ingredient you could build or rebuild your culture around that produced these kinds of actual, measurable results:

• **901% stock price growth (ROI) over 11 years** for organizations that focused on this ingredient in their cultures (vs 74% for those organization that did not over the same 11 years.)

• **Turnover reduction/employee retention…** The AVERAGE annual turnover in the Quick Service Food industry is 170%. The two companies that constantly focus on our magic ingredient more than any other in their cultures average 14% and 24% annual turnover. In other words, these two companies retain their employees 8 to 10 times more than their competitors.

- **Maximizing your success** in providing the ultimate buying experience for your clients, customers, or patients…. According to an exhaustive study by McKinsey, 70% of the buying experience is based upon this ingredient.

- In the past five years, the brand attributes that have become increasingly crucial to buyers are:

Socially responsible:	63% increase
Friendly service:	148% increase
Our magic ingredient:	**391% INCREASE**

- **Profitability:** In the challenging and volatile airline industry, one company has delivered 46 consecutive years of profitability, has had zero layoffs or wage decreases, and averages 3% annual turnover while the industry average is more than 25%. It is the one company in the industry most known and focused on our magical ingredient at the heart of their special culture.

So, what is this magical ingredient? What is at the heart of these spectacular long-term results? *Drumroll…Fireworks…James Earl Jones Narration…*

More than any other single factor, the future success of your organization depends upon …

NESS

"**Kindness costs very little but pays great dividends.**"

S. Truett Cathy – Founder Chick-fil-A

CHAPTER

3

GETTING TO THE
HEART
OF THE MYSTERY

The stunning statistics we just revealed prove beyond any doubt that instilling kindness into the core of an engaging culture is paramount to profitability, service quality, talent retention, and consistent business success. It IS the magic ingredient, the elixir of excellence.

So, here's the trillion-dollar question: *Why haven't more organizations jumped on this opportunity and made the effort and commitment to elevate kindness to the top of their values and to integrate it into the fabric of their culture?* It's right there in front of them (just like Yield signs by the way).

There are two fundamental keys to unlocking this mystery:

1 First is the necessity to breakthrough generations of conditioning about kindness. Until organizations, and especially their top leaders, reject and replace the old misleading conditioning about kindness, they will remain blind to its extraordinary potential. The truth is, though virtually everyone thinks of kindness as a 'good thing,' in business, it has much more often been viewed as 'soft', 'weak,' and 'ineffective.' We've been conditioned to see kindness as the antithesis of the toughness and ruthlessness much more often prized in the business world as vital to gaining power and profits.

"Nice guys finish last." "Only the strong survive in the dog-eat-dog world of business."

This old conditioning is truly an old yellow yield sign! **Success in business today is about** EMPOWER **rather than power;** WE GO **rather than ego.** The real and lasting competitive advantage today is one thing and one thing alone: An extraordinary level of employee engagement driven by a dynamic connecting culture that ignites and sustains such engagement. And, as we've already revealed, kindness more than any other factor generates this kind of successful culture.

2 The second key to unleashing the phenomenal energy of kindness into your organization can only come when you become crystal clear that it is not enough to merely say, "Let's be kind around here." **The essential piece in building kindness effectively into your organization's DNA is to develop and nurture a compelling and dynamic** KINDNESS VALUE PROPOSITION **OR KVP.**

CHAPTER

4

YOUR**K**V**P**

A powerful KVP becomes the GPS for your culture. It gives direction to every customer and teammate interaction. It elevates team spirit and brings purpose to everything each team member does each and every day. Your KVP defines who you are and makes it simple and automatic to do the right things with passion and energy.

Organizations who have instilled their KVP into their culture differentiate themselves from their competitors and achieve exceptional bottom line results and ROI. These few, outstanding organizations have stopped staring at old yellow yield signs and understand that when you change the way you look at people, the people you look at **CHANGE.**

At Chick-fil-A, their KVP is ***"A pleasure to serve."*** It's simple, clear, and memorable. Every Chick-fil-A team member can easily recite those four words to you. But it is the daily, passionate application of this KVP that makes the difference. Chick-fil-A team members WALK this talk, not just talk it! It gives each of them fresh, focused energy. At Chick-fil-A it's not just a job. Their KVP transforms a job into joy; processes into purpose.

Stories of Chick-fil-A team members exemplifying the KVP of "A pleasure to serve" abound and amaze. They've changed flat tires for customers. If it's raining, Chick-fil-A team members are famous for running out to your car with an umbrella and walking you into the restaurant. Customers are always greeted with genuine warmth that makes them feel as if they are truly important and appreciated.

> **"Nearly every moment of every day, we have the opportunity to give something to someone else—our time, our love, our resources."**
>
> *S. Truett Cathy - Founder Chick-fil-A*

One wonderful story really demonstrates how a KVP that is alive and consistently reinforced makes a magnificent difference. One afternoon a regular customer of his local Chick-fil-A was in a bit of a hurry and drove away before receiving his $3.48 worth of change. Now, at pretty much any other quick-service-food restaurant what would you guess would happen to that $3.48?

Odds are very high that it would either go back into the cash register or into the tip jar. But not when you're driven by the KVP of **"A pleasure to serve."** The Chick-fil-A team member placed the change in an envelope with the customer's name on it with a note to be sure he received it when he next came in.

About a week later when that team member handed the previously forgotten $3.48 back to the customer, you can only imagine his amazement. And how many people do you think he told the story to after being treated with such astonishing kindness?

How important is the Chick-fil-A KVP to the bottom-line? We've already seen their unmatched 14% annual turnover rate vs the industry average of 170%. (And, by the way, industry studies reveal that every time a team member must be replaced, the cost to the company is just under $6,000). People love working for a company that centers around a pleasure to serve. But the remarkable results go so much further! A prime measurement of financial success in the quick-service restaurant industry is Average Revenue per Store.

At McDonald's, which for many years set the gold standard, the average revenue per store is $2.7 million annually. Keep in mind that McDonald's stores are open seven days a week and in many locations 24 hours per day.

At Chick-fil-A, even though every single store is closed all day Sundays, THE AVERAGE REVENUE PER STORE IS $4.1 MILLION. KINDNESS WORKS!

At Zappos, their simple but powerful KVP is ***"Delivering Happiness."*** They don't see themselves as a shoe company. They are a PEOPLE company in the business of providing happiness to every customer every single day. Driven by this KVP, Zappos offers free shipping on every single order no matter if the purchase amount is $3 or $3,000. But delivering happiness is not a one-way street. **Zappos ALSO offers free shipping and a 100% money back guarantee for one full year on returns, no questions asked!** It is a level of kindness to their customers that cynics may argue is naïve and bad business policy.

Indeed, many Zappos' customers return more than 50% of the shoes they buy. And, remember, they not only receive all of their money back on those returns, Zappos picks up the tab for shipping. Crazy, right? Not so fast! Zappos has found that these customers who return 50% or more of the shoes they purchase are their most loyal and PROFITABLE customers of all! They return a lot of shoes…but they buy even more.

Maybe kindness isn't such a crazy business strategy.

> **"Every employee can affect your company's brand, not just the front-line employees who are paid to talk to your customers."**
>
> *Tony Hsieh - CEO of Zappo's*

CHAPTER

5

Your **Kindness Value Proposition** is the foundation of a new and rising culture. When top leadership walks their KVP talk, great energy and engagement in the team is ignited. But the speed, acceleration, and ultimate level of success derived from the KVP depends upon the engagement of **EVERY** team member...not just top management. Too many books and teachers still focus only on 'trickle down" as the way to transform a culture. But that is a very outdated yellow yield sign! An unstoppable Kindness culture must be a "360-degree shower" rather than a one-directional trickle.

Your KVP will burst into action and flourish over time only when every single team member assumes the role of Chief Kindness Officer or CKO. To become a CKO requires no tenure, no political savvy, and no advanced degree.

All that is required is focus, heart, and devotion to exemplifying kindness. Every single interaction with a client, teammate, or vendor is a **WOO - Window of Opportunity -** to live up to your title as CKO! And make no mistake, each act of unexpected kindness has the power to ignite a snowball effect as others latch on to that positive kindness energy.

Of course, when the top leaders take personal responsibility to act as CKOs, the acceleration of the Kindness Culture and effectiveness of the KVP will be optimized.

One company in the airline industry has dominated service awards, passenger loyalty, and profitability for the last three decades. It is no coincidence that this airline is widely known for its exceptional culture built upon the cornerstones of fun and kindness. And it is no coincidence that its longtime CEO, who passed away in early 2019 exemplified truly legendary kindness. Of course, that remarkable success story is Southwest Airlines, led for 46 years by the epitome of the CKO, Herb Kelleher.

Herb was famous for his unstoppable love for Southwest team members. He was steadfast in his belief that when your team is motivated by love and kindness rather than fear, the results will be consistently superior. **No wonder that Southwest's home base is called Love Field and their logo is a heart!** Herb demonstrated his devotion to kindness virtually every day throughout his long career at Southwest by surprising his team members as he greeted them by name followed by a big Kelleher hug even when Southwest had grown into an employer of thousands. At the very heart of kindness is irrepressible gratitude. Herb Kelleher showered every Southwest team member with that heartfelt attitude of gratitude.

The results of his extraordinary kindness are indisputable proof that when the CEO takes responsibility to be a CKO astonishing things happen. **Southwest has been profitable for 46 straight years. They've never had a layoff. Their annual turnover rate is less than 3%.** And today, they are the busiest domestic American airline, carrying more passengers each year than any other. Even their policies shine with kindness. They are the only airline that still refuses to charge passengers for checking their bags.

When top leaders embrace the role of CKO, great energy is added to the kindness culture. But it is when EVERY team member steps into those CKO shoes that the KVP gains unstoppable momentum.

"Our people know that if they are sick, we will take care of them. If there are occasions of grief or joy, we will be there with them. THEY KNOW THAT WE VALUE THEM AS PEOPLE, not just cogs in a machine."

Herb Kelleher – Founder of Southwest Airlines

CHAPTER

6

HOW TO
BECOME THE
CKO

Serving as a Chief Kindness Officer is not rocket science. In fact, it is best to adhere to the KISS principle – Keep It Simple Superstar – to master this role. There are seven powerful habits of kindness to develop as a CKO. They are as important at home with family as they are at work with teammates and customers. As you work to build these kindness muscles, they will not only strengthen your relationships with others, they will enhance your own joy, fulfillment, and peace of mind because whenever you seek to enrich another's experience, you can't help but enrich your own! Kindness is the ultimate win-win pursuit.

THE 7 HABITS OF HIGHLY EFFECTIVE CKOS:

1: BEING FULLY PRESENT

When you get right down to it, the key job of the CKO (remember, that's YOU), is to help every person you touch to know they are important. When people feel important and significant, they rise. When people feel taken for granted and unimportant, they fall. But, how do you communicate to others unfakably and un-shakably that they matter, that they ARE important. It all comes down to **the very core of kindness, being fully present.**

When you are fully present for others, 100% of your mind, body, and spirit are with the person you are with, where they are NOW. The result of this simple action has more impact than you can even imagine.

As they so often did when I needed it most, my two daughters, Kelsey and Jenna, became my coaches and taught me a crucial lesson about the unmatched impor-tance of being present for the most precious people in my life.

At the time I was so caught up in my work that I found myself incessantly on the phone or computer trying to iron out a seemingly endless barrage of challenges and concerns. Night after night as my daughters prepared for bed, I'd stop off in my office for "just a moment" to check my voice mail before reading them a story and tucking them in. The next thing I knew, I found myself submerged in dozens of new messages. By the time I finished answering the voice mails, my little girls were sound asleep. I had missed the moment. My wife had read to them, cuddled them, and told them how much their mommy and daddy loved them.

One evening after many weeks of this pattern, Kelsey and Jenna decided it was time to wake their daddy up. They waited patiently in my office doorway until I hung up the phone, then ran over and crawled up into my lap.

Kelsey, who was eight at the time and therefore the spokeswoman said as they both gazed up at me with their beautiful innocence, "Daddy, before we go to sleep, we wanted to ask you something."

"Sure! You can ask anything. What is it girls?"

"Daddy, we just wanted to know, do you love your phone more than you love us?"

These words, so innocently spoken, shot through me, shaking me to my very soul. I had become so accustomed to being busy, so focused on keeping ahead of my voice mail that I had stopped being present for my children. All at once my girls helped me see that only in our moments of fully present connection, do we help those around us build confidence, faith, and self-esteem. It is the only way we fully communicate to them that they are important.

I tucked them in that night and never missed another night unless I was on the road. They taught me that there can be no kindness without presence.

How often does your response to family, friends, or associates begin with "just a minute," "in a second," or "what?" Do you find yourself asking those around you to repeat themselves because you missed their first attempt to communicate with you? When your children or teammates seek your attention, do you often view them as interruptions rather than feeling delight at the opportunity to share some precious moments? These questions can help you to become clear about your level of presence.

If you find yourself falling into any of these patterns, it's an important sign that your focus is drifting away from the present into the past or future. It's time to listen completely before formulating your responses, to turn up your tremendous powers of observation, and to seek to understand others with great kindness, compassion, and unselfishness. As you do you will find your impact on others deepening and your enjoyment of life becoming richer by the moment. You will take an enormous leap towards becoming the CKO you were born to be.

The greatest gift you can give others is something you can offer all year round. Mother Teresa said, "It's not just what we do that makes the difference, it's the love we put into the doing." The love we put into the doing IS the genuine kindness that can only come by being fully present. Give this gift wholeheartedly, determinedly, and joyfully every single day and watch your world expand with more love than you have ever imagined.

"The past is history.
The future...a mystery...
The gift is NOW!
That's why we call it THE PRESENT."

– Eleanor Roosevelt

THE IMPACT OF PRESENCE
IN MOMENTS OF TRUTH

In 1981, Jan Carlzon had just been named the CEO of Scandinavian Airlines. His company was in trouble. They had just been ranked by a consumer poll as the worst airline in the world. Last in service, last in dependability, and last in profits as a percentage of sales. Yet, one year later, in the same poll, they were ranked number one in all three categories. What happened? What was the secret behind this incredible transformation?

Carlzon decided to focus on what he thought was the most critical issue…serving the customer with kindness. He wanted to keep it simple:

IDENTIFY *EVERY* **CONTACT BETWEEN THE CUSTOMER AND EMPLOYEE, AND TREAT THAT CONTACT AS…** "A MOMENT OF TRUTH…" **WITH THE FOCUS ON KINDNESS AND FUN.**

He set out to let every single team member know the importance of that moment…the captain, the ticket agent, the baggage handler, the flight attendant.

"Every moment, every contact," he said, *"must be as pleasant and memorable as possible."*

He figured that he has approximately 10,000,000 customers each year, and on average each customer made contact with five of his people for about 15 seconds apiece. Therefore, in his mind, these 50,000,000 contacts, 15 seconds at a time, would determine the fate of his company.

He set out to share his vision with his 20,000 employees. He knew the key was to empower the front line to be fully present in every 15-second moment of truth. Let them make the decisions and take the actions, because they **WERE** Scandinavian Airlines during those 15 seconds. Through that simple yet incredibly powerful cultural shift, he now had 20,000 people who were energized and ready to go because they were focused on one crucial thing…being fully present…the secret behind making every moment count.

"The moral of the story: perceptions are everything. During each moment you are in contact with a customer, you ARE the organization." *– Jan Carlzon*

THE
7 HABITS
OF HIGHLY
EFFECTIVE
CKOS

2: BLAME BUSTING

There can be no blame in the CKO Hall of Fame! CKOs are dedicated blame-busters! There can be no kindness when blame rears its ugly head. CKOs understand that blame serves no constructive purpose because of its relationship to time.

Is blame about the past, present, or future? Blame is always about the past. So, whenever you find yourself in the act of blaming, you are in the past. Can you do anything about the past? Of course not! Solutions, connection, progress, and kindness are in the present and ignite a better future.

CKOs, as dedicated blame-busters, don't pretend that mistakes or poor decisions aren't made. Instead, they demonstrate kindness when dealing with missteps by immediately bringing everyone into the present moment and moving from **DE**-struction to CON-struction. They simply seek clarity about the actions taken and decisions made and then pivot and ask kindly, "What have we learned and what will we do now to make things better?"

CKOs, by adopting this critical kindness habit of blame-busting, consistently foster cultures where faith overpowers fear of failure. Team members are excited about stepping forward and taking positive risks. They are not afraid to innovate and try different approaches. And, in the business and technological world we live in, accelerating at dizzying rates, this is vital to success. By contrast, in organizations where blame runs rampant, employees feel like the little varmints in the country fair game of Whack-a-mole! They are terrified to stick their necks out for fear they will get bopped on the head.

It's amazing what's accomplished when no one cares who gets the credit. CKOs, as devoted blame-busters **GIVE** credit and take responsibility.

As the legendary Alabama football coach, Paul "Bear" Bryant put so perfectly, **"I'm just an old country plow-hand. But if I've learned one thing about getting a team's heart to beat as one...**

WHEN THINGS GO GREAT,
THEY DID IT.

WHEN THINGS GO PRETTY GOOD...
WE DID IT.

WHEN THINGS GO BAD,
I DID IT."

THE POWER OF BLAME-BUSTING
TO WIN THE HEART

In one of Ronald Reagan's cabinet meetings, General Colin Powell presented an idea he was passionate about. This discussion went on for an hour with Reagan asking tough questions because he felt the proposal had flaws. In the end, however, he said, "Colin, it's your call. If you think it will work, we'll go for it."

A few months later, however, Reagan was grilled at a news conference because the plan had failed miserably. One of the reporters asked the question, "Whose idea was this; yours or someone else's?" Reagan didn't hesitate. He said, "I take full responsibility." He then glanced at Powell sitting in the front row and saw tears welling in his eyes.

After the news conference, Powell walked over to a friend and said, "I'd do anything for that man."

CKOs understand this tremendous power of blame-busting - a kindness practice that wins the heart and builds unmatched loyalty.

"Don't just show kindness
in passing or to be courteous.
Show it in depth, show it with passion,
and expect nothing in return.
KINDNESS IS NOT JUST ABOUT BEING NICE,
IT'S ABOUT RECOGNIZING ANOTHER
HUMAN BEING WHO DESERVES
CARE AND RESPECT."
– General Colin Powell

3: HUMILITY

Perhaps the least appreciated, yet fundamentally most crucial habit to develop as a CKO is genuine humility. For quite some time, it has seemed as if we have been trapped in a relentless hailstorm of ego, defensiveness, and boastfulness. When people must continuously tell us how brilliant, talented, and extraordinary they are, it simply demonstrates that they have an insatiable need for approval rather than actually being brilliant and talented. And when those people are in positions of leadership, they are setting the worst possible examples for those they lead, for their families, and for the future. They are teaching EGO, not We Go! They seem to have lost sight of the incredible impact and magic of authentic humility.

True humility, not the insincere "ah shucks" version that is sometimes used to manipulate others, is inspired by an irrepressible desire to grow, to serve, and improve. It comes from a genuine awe about how much there is to learn every single day everywhere we look. Humility is built from tremendous belief in others, that everyone has something they can teach us by words, ideas, actions, and example.

Humility fosters respect, appreciation, and above all, kindness as we are devoted to help those around us know they are important, significant, and that they can truly make a difference.

> ## "HUMILITY WILL OPEN MORE DOORS THAN ARROGANCE EVER WILL."
> *- Zig Ziglar*

CKOs who exemplify humility seek to build leaders rather than followers and demonstrate the remarkable courage to openly admit when they are wrong or make mistakes. They recognize that these mistakes were not because of intent but rather from interpretations, assumptions, or previous learning that is incorrect, outdated, or no longer applicable. They are much more focused on making things better than on having to be right.

With humility comes appreciation for differences rather than fear. Humble leaders welcome team members with different talents, styles, and perspectives because they understand that those differences become invaluable resources when directed toward benefit for all. They understand as my mentor, the great and humble coaching legend, John Wooden said often when he quoted C.S. Lewis,

"Humility is not thinking less of yourself,
IT'S THINKING OF YOURSELF LESS."

CKOs shine the light of humility to empower others rather than trying to **OVER**power them. Humble leaders as CKOs are far less concerned about demanding loyalty than being loyal to those they lead and serve.

Discover and develop the magic of humility. Be a life-long learner. Have no fear about admitting mistakes. Value differences rather than fearing them. Become easy to impress but hard to offend. Conceit and arrogance are signs of weakness not strength.

Your humility will build more loyalty, energy, and gratitude than bragging and boasting ever will! With humility, your kindness will shine through in every precious moment.

CKO's Understand the Power of HUMILITY

Some people equate humility with weakness. It is just the opposite. Humility is a magnetic force that attracts goodwill from people, and it honors those who possess it. In fact, humility and kindness are joined at the hip.

Think of people who you have met and thought: "Wow! What a wonderful human being!" I can almost guarantee you that their humility made you think that. Humility is not an act but an attitude. It's an attitude of serving and caring for others more than you care about yourself. And those who achieve humility usually are blessed beyond their wildest dreams.

A humble person is always a great listener, and without question, one of the simplest acts of kindness and humility is to listen sincerely to what someone says. I recently heard this great definition for listening: "Listening is wanting to hear." It's an emotional process, not a physical act.

Gallup took a poll of more than one million employees, and of those who thought they had a great boss, guess what was ranked as the number one reason? You got it…their willingness to listen to what you had to say. And I'd be willing to bet if someone took a poll among spouses, you'd get the same result.

CKOs listen because they constantly are seeking to learn. They want to learn because their humility teaches them there is always more to discover, always ways to grow and improve.

> **"Talent is God given. BE HUMBLE.**
> **Fame is man-given. BE GRATEFUL.**
> **Conceit is self-given. BE CAREFUL."**
>
> *- John Wooden*

4: LIVE WITH GRATITUDE

The emotion with the highest frequency and vibration is gratitude. When you come from a place of gratitude, it is absolutely natural and automatic to be kind, to catch others doing things right, and to recognize and appreciate them. You become a "World-Class Buddy-Thanker" who lifts others' spirits and helps them to believe in themselves.

But let me ask an important question. **Who are the people in our lives who we tend to forget to thank the most?** For many, the answer to this question serves as a powerful wake-up call. So often the people we forget to thank the most are the very people who mean the most to us: our family, closest friends, and most important colleagues. We seem to easily fall into the habit of taking these special people in our lives for granted. And, if we're not careful, the spark, joy, kindness, and fun of these most important relationships can begin to fade.

How do you reverse this downward spiral and keep your relationships filled with light and energy? The answer is found in an important CKO strategy: the principle of exaggeration. A simple example will make this principle crystal clear.

In my first career as a United States Swimming coach, a common flaw that many of my swimmers needed to overcome in the freestyle (crawl) stroke was the habit of not pulling far enough under the center of their body where they had the greatest leverage, power, and balance. But, when I attempted to correct swimmers who had developed a wide arm pull by saying: "Pull down the centerline of your body," guess what they said to me in response?

Looking at me as if I needed a strong pair of glasses, they'd reply in total exasperation, "I AM!" They genuinely thought they were pulling properly.

That meant that it did absolutely no good to tell them to pull down the center. Instead, I had to apply the principle of exaggeration. I instructed them to pull as far across their body underwater as they could so the right-hand swept way left under their body, and their left-hand crossed way over to the right.

As soon as they attempted to follow these instructions, guess where they pulled? ZAP! Their stroke now came right down the centerline of their body.

As they exaggerated in this way, how do you think it felt at first? It was strange and uncomfortable. But the more they stayed with it, the more natural and automatic the motion became. Soon they settled into the new and better habit.

Taking those we love and care about for granted and allowing kindness to fade is nothing more than a habit. CKOs can apply the principle of exaggeration to invigorate relationships by becoming "World-Class Buddy-Thankers" just as my swimmers did to transform their strokes.

Writing personal cards to friends, family, and team-mates expressing your gratitude for who they are and what they do, even when it's not their birthday or anniversary is a surprising and impactful strategy CKOs use to deliver kindness. Email, voice mail, text, and social media are fantastic vehicles to share kind thoughts and compliments.

Creating simple unexpected moments of appreciation for others can change the ENTIRE TRAJECTORY OF THEIR LIVES.

"APPRECIATE EVERYTHING YOUR ASSOCIATES DO FOR THE BUSINESS. **NOTHING ELSE** CAN QUITE SUBSTITUTE FOR A FEW WELL-CHOSEN, WELL-TIMED, SINCERE

WORDS OF PRAISE.

THEY'RE ABSOLUTELY FREE AND WORTH A FORTUNE."

Sam Walton – Founder of Wal-Mart

As a CKO and World-Class Buddy-Thanker, you provide great energy and kindness to teammates, customers, and vendors. In all the studies undertaken to examine the effects of recognition and acknowledgment in organizations, not one has been found to have too much.

As a CKO ask yourself every single morning when you awaken, "What am I truly grateful for in my life today?" Instantly you'll remember an important truth that will humble you, inspire you, and fill you with a kind spirit. As the great Olympic champion Wilma Rudolph expressed so perfectly, ***"No matter what great things you accomplish, somebody always helps you."***

KINDNESS AND GRATITUDE–
AN UNSTOPPABLE COMBINATION

William James, one of the founders of modern psychology said, "The deepest principle in human nature is the craving to be appreciated," In fact, a study by Robert Half International found that lack of appreciation was the top reason people leave companies, ahead of money and promotions. Author Michael LeBoeuf says this, "The greatest management principle in the world is…The things that get rewarded and appreciated get done."

What are some creative ways to recognize your people and show them kindness and appreciation?

1. KNOW THEM AS PEOPLE! Find out what's most important to the people you work with. Ask about hobbies, favorite sports, ideal vacations, family, etc. This shows that you're interested in who they are in life rather than just what they do at work.

2. WRITE THE WORD "RECOGNITION" on your desk calendar or enter it as a recurring alert on your cellphone at some regular interval (like every Friday for the entire year). Make this word your trigger to quickly think of people who deserve praise. Then immediately take action to thank them for their positive performance and attitude.

3. NOTIFY THE FAMILY. Send a letter or card to the person's family describing her/his performance and the positive impact it has generated. Hand-written notes and cards are more and more rare. As a result, they carry more and more impact!

4. COMMEMORATE the day a co-worker joined your team. Think about how you'd feel receiving a hand-written card that said something like: "Bob, in case you've forgotten, you came on board here three years ago today. It's a date I won't forget because of all the contributions you've made over these three years. Thank you for being such an important member of the team."

5. ESTABLISH A "WALL OF FAME," both on your website or social media, and in a place of honor at your physical location. Post all kinds of meaningful material: pictures of team members, copies of certificates of completion for training, thank you notes from customers, posts about the organization's success, etc. Let your creativity flow… and be sure to make this an ongoing team project where everyone is encouraged to add ideas and recognize teammates.

For appreciation and recognition to be effective, remember these three things:

- **IT MUST BE GENUINE AND FROM THE HEART**
- **IT MUST BE SPECIFIC**
- **IT SHOULD BE DELIVERED AT ANY TIME, NOT JUST SPECIAL OCCASIONS**

Celebrate with your team whenever and wherever you can. You build teams and people through moments of celebration. It's good for the soul…both yours and theirs.

"IF THE ONLY PRAYER YOU SAID IN YOUR WHOLE LIFE WAS, 'THANK YOU,' THAT WOULD SUFFICE."

– Meister Eckhart

EXPRESS YOUR GRATITUDE AND LIVE PAIN-FREE
By Brian Biro

In the Stephen Spielberg classic film *Always*, Richard Dreyfuss plays a fearless aerial firefighter who is simply the best when it comes to flying bravely into the teeth of raging forest blazes. But when it comes to telling his soul-mate, Holly Hunter, that he loves her, he is a hopeless coward. One day, he pushes the envelope too hard in the attempt to save a group of firefighters trapped by an inferno. Though he somehow manages to rescue them, he cannot pull out from his daring dive and crashes and dies.

The next scene we see is Dreyfuss walking around in confusion about his fate when he runs into Audrey Hepburn, who fittingly in her very last role played an angel glowing with a radiant white light. She informs Dreyfuss that he can't yet go on to heaven because he has left something undone. She tells him, **"The love we fail to share is the only pain we leave with."** Before he can go on to everlasting peace, he must find a way to tell Holly that he truly loves her.

Though I enjoyed the movie up to that scene, Hepburn's words grabbed my heart and shook it. How many of us neglect to tell those we love how we feel until it is too late?

As I thought about those in my own life to whom I had held back my gratitude and love, WHAM, it hit me! The opportunity we all have today as CKOs both personally and professionally is to remember that the love we fail to share is the only pain we LIVE with! When we stop taking those we love and appreciate for granted, we live pain-free! We become World-Class Buddy-Thankers who build people, relationships, teams, and families.

As a CKO, each day you embrace a simple yet powerful truth… you may never pass this way again. So, remember, when you seek to lift others you cannot help but lift yourself. At work, catch your teammates doing things RIGHT, and express your appreciation. At home, look for possibility rather than limits. This attitude of genuine gratitude is the ultimate kindness.

"For beautiful eyes, look for the good in others; for beautiful lips, speak only words of kindness; and for poise, walk with the knowledge that you are never alone." – Audrey Hepburn

5: JUST LISTEN

When I became the vice president of a large training company, our head of customer service felt a great deal of resentment towards me. I had replaced someone she had been extremely loyal to, and she had construed that it was my doing. It was clearly negatively impacting our performance as a team. So, I asked her if she would sit down with me to try something that I knew would, at first, seem a bit unorthodox but that I believed might help us breakthrough. I told her that for ten minutes, I would 'just listen' to her without any interruption, defensiveness, or response. Then after her ten minutes, I asked if she would do the same for me.

I'll never forget her response. She said she didn't think she could talk for ten minutes! I told her how important it was for us to work better together and asked again if she'd give it a try. Deep down inside, she wanted things to improve just as much as I did. So, a bit reluctantly, she said she'd try.

An hour later she stopped talking.

And by the end of that hour, though I didn't say a word, we emerged with an entirely new relationship based on mutual respect and genuine eagerness to work together toward common goals. From that day our team performed at an exciting new level and our friendship and support continues to this day more than 25 years later.

Perhaps the greatest of all human needs is the need to feel **HEARD.** When you listen without focusing on what you're going to say next, you communicate to others that you truly value them.

There is no kinder action you can take. You build trust at the core level. They in turn are much more interested in listening to you. When you truly listen to others, you breakthrough and establish trust far more than by trying to convince them to come over to your way of thinking. You empower rather than overpower.

In our sometimes contentious, self-centered, social media driven world, perhaps it's time to talk less and listen more. It is a powerful secret to begin to replace divisiveness with civility, animosity with understanding, and selfishness with genuine kindness. As the great John Wooden often said, ***"We can disagree without being disagreeable."***

CKOs REMEMBER
THAT WE'VE BEEN
GIVEN TWO EARS
AND ONE MOUTH.

THAT'S A CLUE!

Want to Light a Fire in Others...
Just LISTEN.

By Mac Anderson

Almost thirty years ago I started *Successories,* a company known for selling inspirational wall décor featuring beautiful photos and quotes to reinforce company values and personal goals. I'm pleased to say that it worked. At one point we had over 300 employees, and were shipping over 2,000 framed prints a day. It was fun and fulfilling because we were reinforcing the positive in what can sometimes be a pretty negative world.

I remember it well. One Monday I was walking through the warehouse looking for the shipping supervisor, when I stopped to say hello to Tony, who was busy packing orders. I asked, "Tony, how was your weekend?" He really lit up when he said, "Great! I went fishing with my son." I listened for a few more minutes as he talked enthusiastically about his 12-year-old boy and the fun they had on their fishing trip. Then Tony got back to work.

That night, I was thinking about our conversation and how much I too love to fish. I was smiling as I walked into my closet, remembering the obvious joy Tony felt about the special time with his son when I spotted three of my favorite fishing books on a shelf. Immediately I thought to myself, "I'll bet Tony's son would really enjoy one of these." So, the next day, I found Tony in the warehouse and said to him, "I've got something I think your son will enjoy." Then I handed him the fishing book.

I'll never forget his reaction. You would have thought he had won the lottery! He thanked me profusely, and the next day came to my office to tell me how much his son loved the book. I smiled seeing how happy this little gesture had made Tony and his son, but didn't give it another thought.

But here's the amazing thing… Tony had been a steady, reliable, but relatively unspectacular employee, dutifully picking and packing orders for about three years at the time I gave him the book for his son. Two months later though, Tony's warehouse manager came to my office to inform me that he had promoted Tony to Supervisor. He said something had changed in Tony's attitude over the past two months. The manager told me how Tony had really raised his game, how he had now become a terrific motivator and positive influence with peers, and had taken a leadership role on his own. Tony went on to be one of the best supervisors we ever had.

Although I'm not 100% sure, I have a strong feeling that the gift of that little book, that small unexpected act of kindness made a big difference.

I realize now, all it took was just *LISTENING!*

**"PEOPLE, I'VE LEARNED,
ARE LIKE STICKS OF DYNAMITE...
THE POWER IS ON THE INSIDE,
BUT NOTHING HAPPENS
UNTIL THE FUSE GETS LIT!"**

Mac Anderson – Founder Successories and Simple Truths.

THE
7 HABITS
OF HIGHLY
EFFECTIVE
CKOS

6: ASK MORE THAN TELL

CKOs are *master askers!* This may seem to go against the grain of our typical conditioned view that we go to leaders for answers. But here is a truly liberating truth: **The quality of our teams will be determined by the quality of the questions we ask one another.** CKOs who *ask* more than *tell* ignite leadership qualities and respect in everyone they touch.

As more and more Millennials, GenXers and Gen-Zers fill organizations, a crucial challenge and opportunity is finding the secrets to engage, ignite, and inspire this new workforce. More than ever, it is QUESTIONS rather than answers that can unlock the remarkable potential of these talented generations. It is by learning the fresh skill of becoming a "Master Asker" that you will light up your team with newfound energy, commitment, loyalty, and collaboration. Asking rather than telling is sometimes the ultimate expression of kindness and respect because it is a powerful demonstration of your belief in others.

When we ask questions, we spark creative thought and stimulate discovery. We help others think for themselves. Over time, those we ask rather than tell develop far greater insight and understanding **because we challenge those around us to think for themselves,** which in turn allows their vision to expand. By asking more than telling, we also breathe faith into others' hearts, which helps them build confidence and take responsibility for their decisions and actions.

This doesn't mean there aren't times to give answers. It simply means that as a CKO you want to help others become self-starters who think for themselves and act with confidence and kindness.

A simple strategy for getting started on the path toward becoming a master asker is to discipline yourself to *respond first with a question when people come to you for advice* and answers. Instead of firing off instructions they should take to tackle their problems, first ask, *"What do you think would be the best way to handle this?"* Instantly you've let them know you truly value their ideas, and you've given them the chance to help themselves.

Though initially they may feel somewhat uncomfortable or even disappointed that you didn't give them an answer, **OVER TIME, THE GROWING SENSE OF PERSONAL RESPONSIBILITY YOU WILL FOSTER WITH THIS STRATEGY WILL HELP THEM STRENGTHEN THEIR SPIRITS, SOLUTION-ORIENTATION, AND CONFIDENCE.**

As a CKO, when you ask for a response from someone, it is critical that you **really** listen.

THE SECRET IS TO LISTEN FOR *THEIR* ANSWERS, NOT YOURS.

How many times do we ask questions trying to squeeze out the answer we want? But when you open yourself to really listen, you have a much greater chance to learn.

When you ask others for their ideas, be eager to hear approaches and viewpoints that have never occurred to you before. And welcome those fresh perspectives with genuine enthusiasm, because they have the greatest potential to create positive change in *your* life.

Get the Kindness Train Rolling –
Ask Rather Than Tell

By Mac Anderson

There's a law of science that says at 211 degrees, water is hot… very hot! But at 212 degrees, it boils and turns to steam. And steam can power a locomotive. That one extra degree makes all the difference. In business, I've learned that that one extra degree of kindness can be the difference between good and GREAT.

Great leaders take a 212-degree approach to create a culture of kindness, because they understand that one extra degree can make all the difference with what I call, **UNEXPECTED ACTS OF KIND-NESS.** And often, the most unexpected action leaders can take is to ask instead of tell.

Bruce Black was my partner at McCord Travel. When we sold McCord he stayed on as President with the new owners. He guided the company from $25 million in annual sales to over $600 million in twelve years. McCord became the largest travel company in the Midwest. Bruce was an amazingly kind leader with immeasurable appreciation and respect for his team and who created a 212-degree kindness culture in many ways.

A few years ago, I met a woman at a cocktail party who knew I had been the founder of McCord Travel. Her face lit up when she said she had worked there a few years and loved it! Then she said, "I'll never forget my first day as an account manager. When I arrived, there were two women who greeted me and immediately invited me to join them for lunch." The lunch was great fun, but when she returned to the office, there was a beautiful red rose on her desk and a hand written note from Bruce Black welcoming her to McCord and asking if she would stop by his office around 2:00 p.m. that afternoon.

She met with Bruce for thirty unforgettable minutes. In their time together, not once did he talk about the business or himself. All the conversation was around her! He asked lots of questions about her family, her hobbies, and even her goals and aspirations. And he listened as if she was the most important person in the world! Even today she said, "I get goosebumps just thinking about how special he made me feel."

Asking rather than telling sends an unmistakable message that you are genuinely interested in others...that you respect them...that you truly care about them. It's a message you can carry with you and pass on to others by asking more and telling less.

"PEOPLE DON'T CARE HOW MUCH YOU KNOW UNTIL THEY KNOW HOW MUCH YOU CARE."

Pat Summitt
– Legendary University of Tennessee Women's Basketball Coach

THE 7 HABITS OF HIGHLY EFFECTIVE CKOS

7: FOCUS

One evening my wife and daughters and I were dining in a little café in the Bitterroot Valley in Western Montana where we lived at the time. The café was on the second floor of an old Main Street brick building and had huge windows that captured the stunning panorama of the Bitterroot and Sapphire Mountain ranges enclosing our valley. Everyone in the café was eating or chatting quietly when something caught my four-year-old daughter Jenna's attention and she sprang over to the window. As she gazed out at the mountains a look of pure wonder swept over her and with unbridled excitement and considerable volume she burst out:

"Look Mommy, Daddy, Kelsey... We're in HEAVEN!"

Well, the whole place went dead quiet. Everyone stared at us and we turned bright red. Then, after a moment, the shock gave way to delight, and grins and laughter erupted all around us at the pure joy of Jenna's revelation.

The more I thought about that evening, the more I realized Jenna was brilliant. She had seen the beauty that is always around us, but that most of us pass by without the slightest notice.

WE CAN EASILY MISS THE "HEAVEN" THAT IS RIGHT IN FRONT OF US.
YET OPPORTUNITIES ABOUND IN OUR LIVES WHEN WE REMEMBER TO LOOK FOR THEM.

CKOs look for the heaven in others, the shining new red and white yield signs. They remember that when you change the way you look at people, the people you look at change. As a CKO, when you look for the possibility, the strength, the gifts in others, you do more than find them. You ignite and develop them because what you focus on is what you create.

True kindness is proactive. It requires determined energy. Most of all, it requires focus. It is easy to react with kindness when you are treated kindly. But, CKOs focus on being kind when it's difficult to do so, when people are not being fair, respectful, or positive. CKOs are kind even to the people in their lives they are fairly certain God put them on the planet to test them.

Every great CKO has mastered the Pygmalion Effect, the principle that our thoughts, beliefs, and expectations are magnetic.

Whether verbal or non-verbal, overt or subtle, CKOs, acting everyday as truly positive Pygmalions are able to convey belief in others at key moments that can flip the switch of possibility for them and shoot their lives off in entirely new and exciting trajectories.

What You Focus on is
WHAT YOU CREATE

Seeing true servant leaders in action, guided by their belief in kindness, creates a powerful impact. While I've had the good fortune to meet many successful businesspeople, authors, and speakers during my career, I've never met anyone that walked the talk any more than Ken Blanchard. Over the last forty years, Ken has been extremely successful as a business author. His classic, The One Minute Manager, has sold more than 10 million copies. He has also built a large and very successful training company with the focus on servant leadership, kindness, and extraordinary service.

While visiting Ken at his San Diego office, I learned that one of his employees who worked in his warehouse had recently passed away. Ken had invited the employee's wife to come to his office. When she arrived, he spent over an hour walking around with her carrying a tape recorder to capture all the wonderful memories that other employees had of her husband. When she left, she said it was a day she'd never forget.

You see, what many leaders would have considered an inefficient use of time, Ken saw as the most important aspect of his role as CEO, to serve and thank his people. He didn't do it to look good or because it's expected of him. He did it because he truly cares. It comes straight from his heart, and his team loves him for being a genuine servant leader who understands he can't possibly be a great CEO unless he is first a CKO.

> **"SERVANT LEADERSHIP IS ALL ABOUT MAKING THE GOALS CLEAR AND THEN ROLLING YOUR SLEEVES UP AND DOING WHATEVER IT TAKES TO HELP PEOPLE WIN. IN THAT SITUATION, THEY DON'T WORK FOR YOU, YOU WORK FOR THEM!"**
>
> *Ken Blanchard*

When every member of your team assumes the role of CKO and commits to mastering these seven habits:

- **Being Fully Present**
- **Blame-busting**
- **Humility**
- **Living with Gratitude**
- **Just Listening**
- **Ask More Than Tell**
- **Focus**

you will build a culture filled with unstoppable kindness that will elevate your ROI and profitability, build extraordinary teamwork, loyalty, and cooperation, attract and retain top talent, and ignite everyone on your team to rise to their true potential.

KINDNESS
WORKS!

KINDNESS **STORIES**

Read about some remarkable leaders who exemplify the transformative power of kindness to build people, trust, and extraordinary performance.

Herb Kelleher's legacy is all about love (Herb passed away in January, 2019). Gary Kelly, the current CEO of Southwest Airlines, recalls when he first got hired at Southwest and being impressed at how often Herb used the word "love." He would tell his employees how much he loved them. Not Southwest, not the business…he said, "I love you." Even their home-base in Dallas, TX is called **LOVE FIELD.**

It was widely known that Herb couldn't walk past an employee without saying hello and he never forgot anyone's name. He made each and every person feel as if they were the only person in the room. Herb's impromptu conversations happened so often that his assistants constantly had to intervene to make sure Herb made it to his next meeting, flight, or appointment on-time.

Herb Kelleher regularly demonstrated the ultimate kindness—that he cared deeply about his people. One day, a pair of sisters who worked at Southwest were walking through the lobby of a Houston hospital. They saw Herb talking to a couple of men in suits. They didn't want to bother him and were ready to just move along. But Herb saw them, hollered hello, and came right over to talk. They told him they were there to visit their mother, who had just received bad news about cancer.

Immediately, Herb hustled up to their mother's room and introduced himself as Dr. Kelleher. Then he proceeded to tell their mother how important they were to the airline, and how Southwest Airlines simply could not be who they are without incredible people like her daughters. At that moment, cancer just didn't seem as terrifying.

Herb Kelleher created magical moments like these, every week of every year for 46 years because he loved his people and in turn, they loved him. He was fully present with them, alive with humor, appreciation, and kindness. And with that shining example leading the way, a culture of love, kindness, and fun has ignited

Southwest to become the busiest and most successful airline in the US with less than 3% turnover, countless awards for service, and 46 consecutive years of profits.

"A company is stronger if it it is bound by

LOVE

rather than by fear."

– *Herb Kelleher*

DEAR
Mrs. Johnson

On March 5, 2003, I turned on Good Morning America while eating breakfast. Charlie Gibson was interviewing General Earl Hailston, the commanding general of the U.S. Marines. At the time of the interview, the general was just a few miles from the border of Iraq…waiting to go into battle.

Toward the end of the interview, Gibson asked General Hailston if he had any hobbies outside of his work. The general replied, "Yes, I love photography, especially taking photos of my men and women."

He shared that while he had been waiting for the past few days before moving into battle, he had been taking pictures of his men and women, and at night, he mailed the photos with a brief note to their mothers back in the USA. Charlie asked if he could see one of the letters, and the general walked over, turned on his computer, and read the last letter he had sent. It said:

Dear Mrs. Johnson,

I thought you might enjoy seeing this picture of your son. He is doing great. I also wanted you to know that you did a wonderful job of raising him.

You must be very proud. I can certainly tell you that I'm honored to serve with him in the U.S. Marines.

General Earl B. Hailston

Wow! I had goosebumps as I watched. I then watched as Gibson interviewed a random sample of General Hailston's men and women. You could feel the genuine love and respect that every single one of them had for their leader.

These simple, unexpected acts of kindness given to the families of the men and women for whom he cared so deeply generated unstoppable loyalty and faith. General Hailston truly understood what caring, kindness, and leadership are all about.

FILL YOUR CUP
WITH
KINDNESS

To build a "customer first" culture, you must put them second. Your team members must come first, because there is fundamental truth in business that says, "Your people will only treat your customers as well as they are treated; thus, to have satisfied customers, they must be served by passionate people."

Howard Schultz, the founder of Starbucks, is an extraordinary leader. Early on, Schultz realized that the key to Starbucks' success was to recruit kind and well-educated people who were eager to communicate a real passion for coffee. This, he felt, would be his competitive advantage in an industry where turnover was nearly 200% per year.

To hire the best people, he knew he must be willing to pay them more than the going wage and offer health benefits that weren't available elsewhere. He had seen first-hand with his own parents who suffered many health issues, that the lack of health benefits crippled their family. He saw that part-time people made up two-thirds of his employee base and that no one in the restaurant industry offered benefits to part-timers.

Schultz went to work in an effort to sell his board of directors on increasing benefits while most restaurant executives at the time were looking for ways to cut costs. Initially, Schultz's pleas to investors and his board fell on deaf ears because Starbucks was still losing money. But Schultz was persistent. He was looking long-term and was absolutely committed to growing the young business with kind and compassionate people. Over time, he wore down the board and his investors and convinced them to support providing even his part-time employees with health care benefits. He has said many times over the years that this decision was one of the most important, if not THE most important, that he made at Starbucks. His employee retention rate was about five times the industry average, but even more importantly, he attracted people with great attitudes who loved making their customers feel welcome and at home.

Many times, during his years leading Starbucks, Schultz demonstrated how much he cared about his 'partners' (that's what all team members are called at Starbucks). Early on July 7, 1997, Schultz and his family were asleep at home in East Hampton, NY. The phone rang and he was stunned to learn that three Starbucks partners had been murdered in a botched robbery at a Starbucks store in Washington D.C. He immediately chartered a plane and arrived there before 9:00 AM that morning. He stayed for a week, working with police, meeting with the victim's families, and attending funerals. He ultimately decided that the future profits of the store would go to organizations working for violence prevention and victim's rights.

Howard Schultz understood the power of kindness and compassion. A common quote in the Starbucks family says it all:

"We aren't in the coffee business serving people.
We're in the people business serving coffee."

UNDERSTAND
THE
"SOFT STUFF"

Here's a secret that gives a competitive edge to any leader who really understands it: "The really hard stuff is the soft stuff....it's building a culture around the feelings of your customers and employees." I heard that for the first time a few years ago listening to Tom Asacker, author of *Sandbox Wisdom* as he spoke about building a successful brand. For me, it was one of those "aha" moments that helped put into focus the impact of emotions on behavior.

I heard another memorable quote along those lines not long ago: "You may not remember what someone says or does, but you'll never forget about how they made you feel." This fits so well with Asacker's observation that what customers really care about is how your products or services make them feel about themselves and the buying decision they make.

Mary Kay Ash, the founder of Mary Kay Cosmetics, the sixth largest network marketing company in the world with annual revenues in excess of $3.25 billion, built her highly successful company around this sup-posedly 'soft' concept—the power of feelings. She said two things are more powerful than money and sex... recognition and praise.

Even after she became tremendously successful, ev-ery time she walked into a room, she would pretend that everyone there had a sign around their neck that said, "Please make me feel important." And then she would shower each person she met with kindness, au-thentic appreciation, and energetic praise.

We all want to feel important, to know that we are significant, that we matter. No exceptions!

So, as a leader do you truly understand that the re-ally hard stuff is the soft stuff? Are you building your culture around the feelings of your customers and team members? Are you doing everything you possibly can to make them feel important?

Are you building your culture around kindness and compassion?

"NO MATTER HOW BUSY YOU ARE, YOU MUST TAKE TIME TO MAKE THE OTHER PERSON FEEL IMPORTANT."

– Mary Kay Ash

When Dave Neeleman started the airline Jet-Blue, he knew the importance of leading from the front and letting his actions speak louder than words. His mission was to create a kind-ness culture centered on truly unexpected service, and he knew all eyes would be watching.

A few years ago, I read a great story in INC Magazine written by Norm Brodsky. In the article, Brodsky wrote about being on a JetBlue flight when Neeleman was on board. As we were buckling up to take off, Neeleman stood up and introduced himself. "Hi everyone! I'm Dave Neeleman, the CEO of JetBlue. I'm here today to serve you and I'm looking forward to meeting every one of you before we land."

As he was handing out snacks, he would stop to chat with each passenger. When he came to me, I told him I thought it was a great idea to service his customers first-hand, and asked him how often he did it. Expect-ing him to say once or twice a year, he astonished me when he said, "Not often enough...I get to do it about once a month."

Out of curiosity, I watched him interact with the other passengers. In several instances, I saw him taking notes and listening very intently to what the passengers were saying. A few times, when he couldn't answer a passenger's question, I watched Neeleman take their business card and say, "Someone will be in touch with you in the next 24 hours to answer your question." Even at the end of the flight, there was Neeleman, in his blue apron, leading the charge collecting the trash from the seat pockets.

Now, here's a question for you...Is there any doubt that JetBlue employees knew that their leader was willing to walk the talk when it came to serving the customers with kindness and attention? And, is there any doubt that the front line knew he was on their team?

When asked if he thought leading by example was the most important quality of leadership, the great humanitarian, Albert Schweitzer thought for a second and then replied:

"NO. IT'S NOT THE MOST IMPORTANT ONE. IT'S THE ONLY ONE."

Dave Neeleman, a true CKO, walked that talk.

One of the kindest leaders in history was Mahatma Gandhi. Once when the Mahatma traveled across India preaching peace and nonviolence, a mob of crazed fanatics on horseback rushed his train brandishing spears and clubs, determined to stop the gentle giant by force. Despite the desperate pleas of his aids and supporters, the Mahatma peacefully stepped out onto the train platform and smiled kindly as he looked at the shocked faces of the wild horde.

Then quite calmly, but with a hint of playfulness in his voice he asked, "You have every right to disagree with me - but must you also break my head?"

His humor and kindness in the face of intense anger was so unexpected, so unnerving and disarming to the attackers, that the effect was like a needle puncturing a balloon inflated to the limit. The 'hot air' burst out of them. They stopped in their tracks, lowered their weapons, and quietly rode away.

As a CKO, you will face many times of stress and pressure. One of the most effective tools in your kindness toolkit is a playful, surprising sense of humor.

KINDNESS COMBINED WITH GENTLE HUMOR HAS THE POWER TO
HELP OTHERS LIGHTEN UP
RATHER THAN TIGHTEN UP.

When you can disagree without being disagreeable and shine a light of kindness, you can often turn the tide of negative emotion just as Gandhi turned that frenzied mob.

"In a gentle way,
you can shake the world."

– Mahatma Gandhi

CONCLUSION

The great English writer, Aldous Huxley, was a pioneer in the study of philosophies and techniques to develop human potential. In a lecture toward the end of his life, he said this:

"People often ask me...what is the most effective technique for transforming their lives?"

He then said, "It's a little embarrassing that after years and years of exhaustive research, my best answer is - ***just be a little kinder.***"

This is the paradox of the power of kindness, particularly in business. It doesn't seem to feel powerful at all. In fact, it almost feels too simple to be important. But never forget, simplicity is genius. As Huxley said, "Kindness is the #1 thing that can transform your life."

And now you KNOW, that same simple secret,

KINDNESS,

can transform your brand, your customer loyalty, your success in attracting and retaining fantastic people, and your organization from fear to freedom, from failure to faith, from ego to we go, and from good to GREAT!

"There are three ways to ultimate success:

The first way is to be kind.

The second way is to be kind.

The third way is to be kind.**"**

– Mr. Rogers

BRIAN BIRO is America's Breakthrough Coach. A major client described him best when he said: "Brian Biro has the ENERGY of a 10-year old… the ENTHUSIASM of a 20-year old, and the WISDOM of a 75-year old! Brian has delivered over 1,800 presentations around the world over the last 30 years.

The author of 14 books including his bestseller, *BEYOND SUCCESS,* and his brand new *THE ROI OF KINDNESS,* Brian was rated #1 from over 40 Speakers at 4 consecutive INC. Magazine International Conferences. With degrees from Stanford University and UCLA, Brian has appeared on *Good Morning America,* and *CNN.* Brian was named one of the top 100 most inspirational graduates in the 75-year history of the UCLA Graduate School of Business. He was also honored as one of the top 65 Motivational Speakers in the World. As a member of the Board of Directors for the Kindness for Kids Foundation, Brian is passionate about ending bullying and teaching children the beauty and power of kindness, compassion, and humility.

MAC ANDERSON is the founder of three successful startups… each becoming a leader in its industry. They include Simple Truths, the publishing company; Successories, the leader in marketing products for motivation and recognition; and McCord Travel, the largest travel company in the Midwest.

Most recently, he is the founder of Inspire Kindness where the mission is to start a kindness movement that will have a ripple effect around the world. With Inspire Kindness, he also started the Kindness for Kids Foundation, which funds kindness campaigns in grade schools so kids will be less likely to bully once they get to middle school and beyond.

Mac has also spoken to many corporate audiences on a variety of topics including leadership, motivation, team building and this new topic, the R.O.I of Kindness. As an author he has written or co-authored 24 books that have sold over 4 million copies including his bestsellers, *212 One Extra Degree* and *You Can't Send a Duck to Eagle School*.

EXPERIENCE THE IMPACT KINDNESS CAN HAVE IN YOUR ORGANIZATION!

The ROI of Kindness is a new and innovative education and training program dedicated to helping corporations drive bottom-line returns by building and enhancing a culture of kindness.

- *Book a Keynote Speaker*
- *Schedule a Live Webinar*
- *Set Up an Interactive Workshop*

For more information, visit **roiofkindness.com** or call **877.935.6357.**